MERSEYSIDE BUSES
1986–2004

KEITH A. JENKINSON

AMBERLEY

First published 2023

Amberley Publishing
The Hill, Stroud
Gloucestershire, GL5 4EP

www.amberley-books.com

Copyright © Keith A. Jenkinson, 2023

The right of Keith A. Jenkinson to be identified
as the Author of this work has been asserted in
accordance with the Copyrights, Designs and
Patents Act 1988.

ISBN 978 1 3981 0958 2 (print)
ISBN 978 1 3981 0959 9 (ebook)

British Library Cataloguing in Publication Data.
A catalogue record for this book is available from
the British Library.

Origination by Amberley Publishing.
Printed in the UK.

Introduction

Merseyside was created as a metropolitan county on 1 April 1974 as a result of the Local Government Act 1972 and comprises the boroughs of Knowsley, St Helens, Sefton, Wirral and the city of Liverpool. Prior to this, on 1 December 1969 Merseyside PTE had come into operation when Liverpool, Wallasey, and Birkenhead Corporations buses were placed under its control as Merseyside Transport, and the services of NBC subsidiaries Crosville and Ribble were coordinated. Later, following the local government reorganisation on 1 April 1974, St Helens and Southport Corporation bus operations were also absorbed into Merseyside PTE.

After establishing a corporate livery based on that of the erstwhile Liverpool Corporation, in 1986 the PTE was reformed as an arm's-length company under the title Merseybus and the livery was changed to maroon and cream. All was set to change, however, when the deregulation of local bus services took place on 26 October 1986 and the PTE suddenly faced competition from a number of independent operators, some of whom were established coach companies while others were total newcomers to the industry. Earlier in the year, the NBC had split part of the large Ribble empire into three parts, one of which became North Western, who took over its operations from its Aintree and Bootle depots, as well as its Wigan and Manchester bases. Later sold to Drawlane in 1988, North Western passed to British Bus and then the Cowie Group, which was rebranded Arriva in 1997. Similarly, the NBC divided Crosville into two separate companies – Crosville Wales and Crosville, with the latter passing to the ATL group in 1988 – and then in 1989 to Drawlane, which, as said earlier, three years later was restructured as British Bus. However, in the meantime, in February 1990 Drawlane had sold its Wirral and Chester operations to PMT, who maintained the Crosville name, albeit on its yellow and red fleet livery, despite soon after deregulation having established a base on the Wirral at Moreton from which it had begun services under its Red Rider brand. Following its acquisition by Badgerline, and then FirstBus, PMT was rebranded as First Crosville into which its Red Rider operation was absorbed.

Over the next few years, while some of the new independent operators failed to achieve success and quietly disappeared, several others entered the fray and built up sizeable fleets. As was perhaps to be expected, however, by the mid-1990s some of these had sold their businesses to the larger concerns, and in an attempt to stem the newcomers efforts, after having adopted some local brand names in St Helens, Southport and the Wirral Penninsula, Merseybus also set up some low-cost units.

Early in 1993, Merseybus was sold to its management through an ESOP scheme and changed its title to MTL Trust Holdings. Seeing the need for a major fleet update, one of its first moves was to strike a deal with London Buses for the purchase, over two years, of 250 mid-life Leyland Titans, a large number of which were quickly placed in service still wearing the livery of their former owner. Following this and looking for expansion, MTL began operating some services in Manchester which competed with GM Buses. The latter, however, being unhappy with this, quickly retaliated in Liverpool, Southport and the Wirral, and in the latter adopted a new livery similar to that previously used by Birkenhead Corporation and applied a Birkenhead and District fleet name. Ultimately, after both companies found their new operations to be highly unprofitable, an agreement was reached in 1995 under which they returned to their established territories. In the meantime, in 1993 MTL had acquired its competitor, Fareway Passenger Services, and over the next two years purchased Liverbus and Blue Triangle, the latter of which was merged into MerseyRider while the other two were, for a few years, kept as separate entities. In addition, Liverline was purchased by Drawlane in 1993 and merged into North Western, who retained its identity for a number of years, Citybus was taken over by Lynton Travel in July 1993, St Helens based South Lancashire Transport was acquired by the Cowie Group in 1997, and then Village Group sold its bus operations to MTL in March 1998.

As is well known, in November 1997 the Cowie Group was rebranded as Arriva and adopted a new national corporate livery and identity, which quickly began to replace MTL's colours. Already owning North Western when Arriva purchased MTL in 2000, this put it in a dominant position on Merseyside, and in particular in Liverpool, and as such it was instructed by the Competition Commission to dispose of part of its new empire. As a consequence, it ultimately, and reluctantly, agreed to sell its Gillmoss depot and its operations, these being purchased in July 2001 by a new company, Glenvale Transport Limited (GTL), which inherited an elderly fleet of buses in urgent need of replacement.

Despite the demise of the aforementioned private operators, throughout the 1990s independents on both sides of the Mersey had continued to compete with MTL, with some growing considerably and improving their fleets with new buses, and others ultimately taking the decision to withdraw from the fray and quietly disappear or return to their coaching roots. In the meantime ABC Buses at Formby was acquired by Aintree-based CMT in 1998, who remained independent until June 2003 when it was purchased by GTL, who was later acquired by Stagecoach in July 2005.

Over the years since deregulation, Merseyside has always been a fascinating area for bus enthusiasts with variety abounding, and although I have illustrated a large number of the operators that were to be seen between 1986 and 2003, several unfortunately escaped my camera on my visits across the Pennines from my native Yorkshire, and for this omission I apologise. I do, however, hope that the following photographs evoke memories of the past, and that you will enjoy seeing them.

Resting in the yard of Merseyside PTE's Gillmoss depot on 20 August 1973 is Crossley-bodied Leyland PD2/20 L334 (VKB 855), which began life with Liverpool Corporation in September 1957. (K. A. Jenkinson)

Amongst the last buses to enter service with Birkenhead Corporation, Northern Counties-bodied Leyland PDR1A/1 176 (MBG 376H), which was new in November 1969, is seen here wearing its new owner's livery and fleet name. (K. A. Jenkinson)

Seen at Thurstaston while operating a private hire on 11 July 1986 are Leyland National 6027 (SKF 27T) and Alexander-bodied Leyland AN68/1R 1450 (GKA 450L), both of which were new to Merseyside PTE in June 1979 and May 1973 respectively. (K. A. Jenkinson)

Displaying a Merseymini fleet name in Southport on a wet 14 July 1987 is Merseyside PTE Dodge Northern Counties-bodied Dodge S56 7707 (D707 TWM), which was at the time only two weeks old. (K. A. Jenkinson)

With three Merseyside PTE and one Ribble buses forming the backdrop in Liverpool city centre,
NBC subsidiary Crosville's ECW-bodied Bristol VRT DVL382 (FTU 382T) is seen here on the
H5 service to Warrington. (K. A. Jenkinson)

Displaying NBC and Merseyside PTE logos alongside its fleet name is Ribble's Park Royal-bodied
Leyland AN68/1R, which was new to the company in January 1974. (K. A. Jenkinson)

Heading out of Southport on its way to Preston on 14 July 1987 is Ribble Leyland National 697 (SCK 697P), which was new in August 1976 and is seen here in its owner's post-NBC livery. (K. A. Jenkinson)

Seen in Liverpool awaiting its departure back to Wigan on the 320 service is GM Buses Northern Counties-bodied Leyland AN68A/1R 8416 (SND 416X), which was new in August 1981 and displays a local Wigan logo. (K. A. Jenkinson)

Resting in Southport in August 1988 is Merseybus Duple-bodied Dennis Lancet 7030 (EKA 230Y), which began life with the PTE in May 1983. (K. A. Jenkinson)

Seen in Southport operating the circular tour on 14 June 1989 is Merseybus open-top Weymann-bodied Leyland PD2/40 0651 (CWM 151C), which started life with Southport Corporation as a conventional covered-top bus in July 1965. (K. A. Jenkinson)

Laying over in Bootle in August 1988 is North Western 12 (D212 SKD), an Alexander-bodied Mercedes Benz L608D which was new to the company in September 1986. (K. A. Jenkinson)

Wearing the old and new Merseybus livery and seen in Water Street, Liverpool, are Alexander-bodied Leyland AN68/1R 1566 (PKB 566M) and East Lancs-bodied Leyland AN68A/1R 1737 (LKF 737R), which were new in July 1974 and February 1977 respectively. (K. A. Jenkinson)

Painted in an experimental livery, Merseybus Alexander-bodied Leyland AN68D/1R 1955 (ACM 755X) is followed down Water Street, Liverpool, by its sister from 1957 (ACM 757X), which wears its owner's new maroon and cream colour scheme. (K. A. Jenkinson)

Resting at its depot on 8 October 1989 is North Western ECW-bodied Leyland 523 (FBV 508W), which was new to Ribble in September 1981. (K. A. Jenkinson)

New to North Western in May 1987, Carlyle-bodied Freight Rover Sherpa 80 (D80 TLV) is pictured here at its owner's Aintree depot on 8 October 1989. (K. A. Jenkinson)

Starting life with Southdown in April 1966, Northern Counties-bodied Leyland PD3/4 932 (FCD 295D) is seen here near Pier Head, Liverpool, on 14 June 1989 while being used by North Western as a driver training bus. (K. A. Jenkinson)

Operating the 222 Albert Dock Circular service, for which it is branded, is Crosville Dormobile-bodied Freight Rover Sherpa MSR739 (D739 PTU), seen here in Liverpool city centre on 14 June 1989. (K. A. Jenkinson)

Approaching Pier Head, Liverpool, on 14 June 1989, and wearing Crosville's post-NBC livery, is ECW-bodied Leyland Olympian DOG151 (A151 UDM), which was then five years old. (K. A. Jenkinson)

Purchased new by Merseyside PTE in November 1974, East Lancs-bodied Bristol VRT GKA 60N is seen here on 8 October 1989 after being acquired by independent Fareway, in whose fleet it was numbered 101. (K. A. Jenkinson)

Also starting life with Merseyside PTE was 1972-vintage Alexander-bodied Leyland PDR1A/1 BKC 290K, seen here approaching Pier Head, Liverpool, on 8 October 1989 after passing to Amberline. (K. A. Jenkinson)

Parked in the yard of Merseybus's Southport depot on 8 October 1989 is Duple-bodied Leyland Tiger 7010 (CKC 625X), which carries a Merseycoach fleet name. (K. A. Jenkinson)

Heading down Water Street, Liverpool, on 14 June 1989 is Merseybus Alexander-bodied Leyland AN68D/1R 1938 (ACM 738X), which had been new to Merseyside PTE in December 1981. (K. A. Jenkinson)

Purchased new by Amberline in July 1992, Wright-bodied Mercedes Benz 709D J735 MFY is seen here in central Liverpool when four months old. (K. A. Jenkinson)

New to London Transport in July 1975, MCW-bodied Daimler CRL6 GHM 874N is seen here in Liverpool operated by local independent Coleman with its destination on a board below its windscreen. (K. A. Jenkinson)

Blue Triangle's ECW-bodied Leyland Leopard PSU5E/4R 36 (UDW 639Y), which had been new to National Welsh in November 1982 registered PKG 105Y, is pictured here in central Liverpool in 1993 followed by a GM Buses Leyland Atlantean, which was competing on the 79 service to Croxteth with Merseybus, one of whose ex-London Leyland Titans is also visible. (K. A. Jenkinson)

Originating with Tyne & Wear PTE in June 1979 but then serving with London Buses, MCW Metrobus VRG 416T is seen here in December 1993 immediately after being acquired by Merseybus still sporting a London Northern fleet name above its destination screen but with a Merseybus logo on its side panels. (K. A. Jenkinson)

Starting life in February 1987 with D-Coaches, Morriston in South Wales, and then operating for Scottish independent Whitelaw of Stonehouse, Leyland Lynx D32 MWN is seen here turning on to Strand, Liverpool, in 1996 after being acquired by Citybus, Toxteth. (K. A. Jenkinson)

Immaculately presented and belying its age, Powney of Aintree's City Fleet ECW-bodied Bristol VRT UMB 337R, seen here on a journey to Garston in the summer of 1992, was new to Crosville in February 1977. (K. A. Jenkinson)

Buses of numerous different operators congregate in Liverpool's Hood Street bus terminal in 1992. (Author's collection)

New to West Yorkshire Road Car Co. in December 1974 but acquired by Liverline from Halton Transport, Leyland National 03 (GUG 120N) heads through Liverpool city centre on a quiet Sunday morning in 1993. (K. A. Jenkinson)

Merseybus Willowbrook-bodied Leyland AN68B/1R 1866 (AFY 186X), which was new in December 1981, is seen here resting in Pier Head bus station, Liverpool. (K. A. Jenkinson)

Still wearing the red livery of London Buses from whom it was acquired in May 1993, but adorned with a Merseybus fleet name and number while still retaining its London fleet number, Leyland Titan KYV 417X is seen here traversing The Strand, Liverpool, in July 1993. (K. A. Jenkinson)

Merseyside PTE's low-cost unit Mersey Rider's Carlyle-bodied Mercedes Benz 811D 7950 (G950 RFL), which started life with Cambus in June 1990, heads through Liverpool city centre followed by Merseybus Alexander-bodied Leyland AN68/1R 1570 (PKB 570M). (K. A. Jenkinson)

Also acquired from Cambus and seen in Liverpool in 1993 is independent Fairway's Northern Counties-bodied Leyland FE30AGR 119 (OBN 509R), which had been new to Lancashire United in May 1977. (K. A. Jenkinson)

Acquired by North Western from Amberline in 1993 and seen here later that year still in its former owner's livery, MCW-bodied Leyland FE30ALR 576 (NOC 382R) had begun life with West Midlands PTE in September 1976. (K. A. Jenkinson)

Seen operating the cross-Mersey 433 service from Liverpool to New Brighton in 1993 is Avon Buses ex-London Buses Leyland Titan CUL 96V, which was new in January 1980 and purchased by its new Prenton, Wirral, owner in November 1992. (K. A. Jenkinson)

Turning into Castle Street, Liverpool, on 16 June 1993 is Liverbus Park Royal-bodied Leyland AN68A/1R 52 (UNA 851S), which was new to Greater Manchester PTE in December 1977. Behind it is one of GM Buses Atlanteans, which was competing with Merseyside PTE on route 79. (K. A. Jenkinson)

New to London Country in August 1978, Park Royal-bodied Leyland AN68A/1R, Liverline 73 (XPG 159T) is seen entering Castle Street, Liverpool, en route to Halewood on 16 June 1993. (K. A. Jenkinson)

Purchased new by Liverbus in April 1993, Northern Counties-bodied Volvo B10B 101 (K101 OHF) is seen here on the 275 service to Huyton when only two months old. (K. A. Jenkinson)

Collecting its Fazakerley-bound passengers in July 1993 is Blue Triangle of Bootle's former Western SMT Alexander-bodied Ailsa B55 59 (KSD 112W), which started life with Western SMT in November 1980. (K. A. Jenkinson)

Standing at The Plaza development, Pier Head, Liverpool, a few months before its withdrawal in 1993, is Merseybus Alexander-bodied Leyland AN68/1R 1304 (DKC 304L). (K. A. Jenkinson)

Turning into Castle Street, Liverpool, on 16 June 1993 is Garston-based Merseyline Travel's MCW-bodied Leyland FE30AGR SDA 772S, which had begun life with West Midlands PTE in March 1978. (K. A. Jenkinson)

Seen in Queen Square bus station, Liverpool, while operating the long service from Chester to Southport in 1993, is PMT/Crosville's coach-seated ECW-bodied Leyland Olympian EOG200 (B200 DTU). (K. A. Jenkinson)

Merseybus's low-cost unit, Mersey Rider's 1976-vintage East Lancs-bodied Leyland AN68A/1R 1713 (JWM 713P), passes through Liverpool city centre on its way to Halewood in 1993. (K. A. Jenkinson)

Wearing Merseybus subsidiary's Fareway livery is Leyland National 7001 (RKA 886T), which was new to Merseyside PTE in December 1998, seen here on The Strand en route to Northwood on 9 April 1994. (K. A. Jenkinson)

Painted North Western's short-lived Red Knight low-cost unit's livery in 1993 is Park Royal-bodied Leyland PDR1A/1 478 (JPL 190K), which was new to London Country in October 1972. (K. A. Jenkinson)

Looking immaculate as it makes its way along Dale Street, Liverpool, on 17 June 1993 is Carlyle-bodied Freight Rover 350D F202 XBV, which was purchased new by ABC, Ainsdale, in January 1989. (K. A. Jenkinson)

Liverbus's Willowbrook-bodied Leyland PSU5/4R GDM 996X, seen here in Dale Street, Liverpool, on 17 June 1993, has a fascinating history. Starting life in May 1971 with Biss, Bishop's Stortford registered VUR 217J and fitted it with a Van Hool coach body. In 1981 it was given a new Duple III body by Barry Cooper, Warrington, and re-registered GDM 996X. Then after passing to Liverbus it gained its current body in August 1992. (K. A. Jenkinson)

Operated by Liverline on behalf of Merseytravel and branded for the 224 service, Ikarus-bodied DAF SB220 J414 NCP is seen here traversing Dale Street, Liverpool, on 17 June 1993. (K. A. Jenkinson)

New to Burnley & Pendle in September 1976, Garston-based independent Village Group's East Lancs-bodied Bristol VRT URN 153R is seen here in Dale Street, Liverpool, on 17 June 1993. (K. A. Jenkinson)

One of several former London Transport Leyland FE30AGRs purchased by Fareway Passenger Services, Kirkby, MCW-bodied 152 (OJD 245R), which was new in July 1977 and is seen here in Dale Street, Liverpool, on 17 June 1993, arrived on Merseyside in September 1988 after having served with Hampshire Bus and Cumberland following a mere six years of service with its original owner. (K. A. Jenkinson)

Seen in Water Street, Liverpool, en route to Lyme Cross, Alexander-bodied Dennis Dominator 0035 (ACM 768X) was new to Merseyside PTE in February 1982. (K. A. Jenkinson)

Starting life with Crosville in January 1984 registered A43 SMA, North Western 823 (1205 FM) is a Duple-bodied Leyland Tiger to which an ugly home-made front end has been fitted. (K. A. Jenkinson)

During the conflict between Merseybus and GM Buses, MTL East Lancs-bodied Leyland AN68A/1R 1738 (LKF 738R) is seen heading down Shaw Road, Oldham, on its way to Manchester on 27 October 1993. (K. A. Jenkinson)

Northern Counties-bodied Leyland Olympian 3281 (F281 DRJ) is seen here sporting the green between decks band applied to several of the GM Buses double deckers used on the retaliative services in Liverpool during 1993 to 1995. (K. A. Jenkinson)

An older GM Buses Leyland used in Liverpool on the 79 service was 1983-vintage Northern Counties-bodied AN68D/1R Atlantean 4655 (ANA 955Y), seen in Liverpool on its way back from Kirkby in 1993. (K. A. Jenkinson)

Displaying 'The Friendly Bus' lettering on its front and side panels when caught by the camera in October 1993 is CMT's Leyland National UFG 61S, which began life with Southdown in September 1977. (Author's collection)

Seen in St Helens operating a tendered PTE service is South Lancs ex-National Welsh Carlyle-bodied Freight Rover 405D G282 HDW, which was new in January 1990. (K. A. Jenkinson)

Entering The Strand, Liverpool, on 16 June 1993 are two ex-London Leyland Titans headed by 2339 (KYV 339X), which had only been acquired a few weeks earlier and was still in the livery of its former owner, albeit now sporting Merseybus fleet names and number plate. (K. A. Jenkinson)

Seen at MTL's Gillmoss depot, Liverpool, on 9 April 1994, wearing different liveries are Leyland Titans 2269 (GYE 269W), 2425 (KYV 425X), 2746 (OHV 746Y) and 2350 (KYV 350X), all of which originated with London Transport. (K. A. Jenkinson)

Freshly repainted into Merseybus livery is former London Leyland Titan 2385 (KYV 385X), which was acquired in May 1993 but had begun life in the capital in December 1981. (K. A. Jenkinson)

Freshly repainted and given its new fleet number 505 ready for its transfer to MTL's London Suburban Buses operation is former London Buses Leyland Titan CUL 187V, seen here at Queen Square bus station, Liverpool, in August 1993. (K. A. Jenkinson)

Wearing MTL livery with Southport fleet names, Leyland National 2 6107 (VBG 107V), which was new to Merseyside PTE in July 1980, is seen here on Lord Street, Southport, on 15 September 1994. (K. A. Jenkinson)

With park & ride lettering and Southport fleet name, MTL Plaxton-bodied Volvo B6 7201 (L201 TKA) awaits its passengers at the Monument, Southport, on 16 September 1994 when only four months old – the bus, of course, and not the monument. (K. A. Jenkinson)

MTL Southport-liveried East Lancs-bodied Leyland AN68A/1R 1821 (RBG 821T), which was new to Merseyside PTE in May 1979, rests at the Monument, Southport, on 16 September 1994. (K. A. Jenkinson)

Starting life with Viscount, Peterborough, in September 1989, MTL Southport's Optare StarRider-bodied Mercedes Benz 811D 7944 (G804 OVA) stands at the Monument, Southport, on 16 September 1994. (K. A. Jenkinson)

On a damp September 1994 day, GM Buses North's ex-South Wales MCW Metrorider 1586 (D260 PEP) heads along Lord Street, Southport, on a service that was competing with MTL Southport. (K. A. Jenkinson)

Also competing with MTL Southport on 16 September 1994 was GM Buses North's Northern Counties-bodied Leyland Olympian 3243 (C243 EVU), seen here on the town's Lord Street followed by MTL Southport's park & ride-liveried Plaxton-bodied Volvo B6 7202 (L202 TKA). (K. A. Jenkinson)

New to Bee Line Buzz Company, Manchester, but seen here in Liverpool in North Western livery is Northern Counties-bodied Scania L113CRL 1045 (P45 MVU). (K. A. Jenkinson)

Being restored by Blue Triangle inside its Bootle depot on 9 April 1994 is MCN30K, a 1958 Metro Cammel-bodied Leyland PD3/4 that had been converted by Northern General into normal control layout in April 1972 and was semi-preserved. Alongside it undergoing attention is ex-Western SMT Alexander-bodied Ailsa B55 KSD 112W. (K. A. Jenkinson)

Standing in the yard of Merseybus's Gillmoss depot on 9 April 1994 are ex-London Buses Leyland Titan 2073 (CUL 73V) and MCW Metrobus 2417 (VRG 417T), which originated with Tyne & Wear PTE and are both still in their former operator's livery, and MCW Metrobus GBU 10V, which had recently been acquired from Stevensons, Spath, in whose colours it is seen here. (K. A. Jenkinson)

Collecting two passengers in St Helens is South Lancs Transport Plaxton-bodied Dennis Dart J8SLT, which had been purchased new by the company in July 1992. (K. A. Jenkinson)

During the 1990s, Aintree-based independent CMT operated a large fleet of second-hand Leyland Nationals, one of which, JBO 351N, was new to Cardiff City Transport in June 1975 and is see here in Liverpool city centre. (K. A. Jenkinson)

Purchased new by Little White Bus, Aughton, in May 1988, Northern Counties-bodied Dodge S56 E224 BVR is seen here in Southport on its service to Ormskirk on 15 September 1994, soon after which the company was acquired by North Western. (K. A. Jenkinson)

When GM Buses competed with Merseybus on the Wirral, it repainted its vehicles into a livery similar to that used by Birkenhead Corporation prior to it being subsumed into the PTE. Illustrating this, and sporting Birkenhead & District fleet names, is GM Buses Northern Counties-bodied Leyland FE30AGR 4098 (BVR 98T), which had started life with Greater Manchester PTE in May 1979. (K. A. Jenkinson)

Seen in Liverpool in October 1995 on its owner's service to Runcorn is Warrington Transport's eight-month-old Plaxton-bodied Dennis Dart 238 (M238 YKD), which carries MidiLines fleet names. (K. A. Jenkinson)

Looking immaculate and freshly repainted into Merseybus's low-cost Mersey Rider livery is East Lancs-bodied Leyland AN68A/1R 1704 (JWM 704P), which began life with Merseyside PTE in June 1976. (K. A. Jenkinson)

St Helens-based Merseybus Northern Counties-bodied Leyland Olympian 0258 (F258 YTJ) is seen here fitted with local Lancashire Travel fleet names. (K. A. Jenkinson)

Adorned with a St Helens depot code sticker in its windscreen and Lancashire Travel fleet names is Merseybus Leyland National 2 6082 (VBG 82V), which was new to Merseyside PTE in June 1980 and is seen here in Wigan bus station. (K. A. Jenkinson)

Seen in Liverpool wearing an anonymous white livery with low-cost unit 'No Fuss Bus' lettering is North Western Leyland National 461 (OAH 552M), which began life with Eastern Counties in October 1973. (K. A. Jenkinson)

Sandwiched between ex-Merseyside PTE Alexander-bodied MCW Metrobus 0059 (DEM 759Y) and former London Leyland Titan 2211 (CUL 211V) at Gillmoss depot on 9 April 1994 is MCW Metrobus 3076 (JBO 76W), which had been acquired by MTL from South Wales municipal Newport Transport. (K. A. Jenkinson)

Entering Queen Square bus station, Liverpool, and wearing 'Silver Service' branding on its lower side panels and route details above is Merseybus coach-seated Alexander-bodied Leyland Olympian 0064 (A316 GLV), which was new in October 1983. (K. A. Jenkinson)

Bussco was a tiny independent who later became Online Travel. Here its former Ribble Leyland National UHG 737R is seen heading down Lime Street, Liverpool, past St George's Hall. (K. A. Jenkinson)

Displaying North Western Liverline fleet names, Northern Counties-bodied Scania N113DRB 675 (G38 HKY) started life with the independently owned Liverline in January 1990. (K. A. Jenkinson)

New to Merseyside Trust Holdings in August 1996 and seen here with 'SMART' branding and an MTL logo on its cove panels, and route branding and Merseybus fleet name on its lower side panels, is Wright-bodied Scania L113CRL 5310 (P310 HEM). (K. A. Jenkinson)

Unusual buses to be purchased by a PTE were six Locomotor-bodied twenty-three-seat rear-engined Quest Bs for Merseyside PTE in 1985. One of these – B930 KWM – is seen here in St Helens in 1994 on route 7 to Prescot after being acquired by local independent Tanner. (K. A. Jenkinson)

Seen here in St Helens bus station is locally based independent Hattons Leyland National EBG 83T, which had started life north of the border with Central SMT in January 1979. (K. A. Jenkinson)

Fitted with a wheelchair lift in its centre door and painted in Merseytravel livery is CMT Leyland National WFM 810L, which started life with Crosville as a conventional dual-door bus in September 1972. (K. A. Jenkinson)

Merseybus Duple-bodied Dennis Lancet 7024 (EKA 224Y) with Lancashire Travel fleet names rests in St Helens bus station after having completed a local service. (K. A. Jenkinson)

Seen in its home town bus station in 1994 wearing St Helens Rider fleet names is Merseybus Optare StarRider-bodied Mercedes Benz 811D 7941 (G801 OVA), which began life with Viscount, Peterborough, in September 1989. (K. A. Jenkinson)

Picture operating a school service in St Helens in 1994 is Merseybus East Lancs-bodied Leyland AN68A/1R 1825 (RBG 825T) wearing local St Helens Rider livery and fleet name. (K. A. Jenkinson)

New to South Midlands in June 1987, Optare City Pacer D231 TBW is seen here seven years later in St Helens bus station operated by local independent Pugh, who used Town Flyers as its fleet name. (K. A. Jenkinson)

Seen in Southport suitably lettered for its driver training role is MTL Alexander-bodied Leyland PDR1A/1 1263 (BKC 263K), which was new to Merseyside PTE in May 1972. (K. A. Jenkinson)

Nicely repainted into MTL's Merseybus livery is Alexander-bodied Leyland AN68D/1R 1034 (A114 HLV), which was new to Merseyside PTE in February 1984 and is seen here on 25 September 1996. (K. A. Jenkinson)

New to Eastern National in March 1985, a coach-seated ECW-bodied Leyland Olympian, originally registered B694 BPU, is seen here at Edge Lane depot, Liverpool, on 25 September 1996 after joining MTL's Sightseers coaching fleet, in which it was numbered 0507 and re-registered A12 MTL. (K. A. Jenkinson)

Starting life in January 1975 as a conventional closed-top bus with Merseyside PTE, Alexander-bodied Leyland AN68/1R 1612 (GKA3 7N) was converted to open top for use at Southport where it is seen here on 23 September 1996. (K. A. Jenkinson)

Resting at the depot of its owner, Village Group, in 1995 is much travelled ex-London AEC Routemaster EDS537B (originally 630 DYE), which had been purchased in November 1994. (K. A. Jenkinson)

Seen in Liverpool city centre en route to Toxteth on route 100 is MTL MerseyRider's Marshall-bodied Mercedes Benz 811D 7948 (K948 OEM), which was new in February 1993. (K. A. Jenkinson)

Heading along Victoria Street, Liverpool, displaying Merseybus and Wirral Penninsula fleet names, is Ikarus-bodied DAF SB220 6330 (K130mTCP), which had been purchased new in July 1993. (K. A. Jenkinson)

New to Merseyside PTE in March 1981 but seen here passing St George's Hall, Liverpool, in September 1996 sporting Liverbus fleet names, is Leyland National 2 6142 (XLV 142W). (K. A. Jenkinson)

Seen in Liverpool city centre in September 1996 is Citybus Leyland National 2 LUA 325V, which was new to West Yorkshire PTE in March 1980. (K. A. Jenkinson)

Heading down Lime Street, Liverpool, past St George's Hall on its way to its home town in October 1996, is Warrington Transport East Lancs-bodied Dennis Dominator 95 (F95 STB). (K. A. Jenkinson)

Starting life with Plymouth City Transport in January 1978, Roe-bodied Leyland AN68A/1R OCO 107S was latterly operated by Bee Line Buzz Company before passing to North Western's Liverline subsidiary, who retained its fleet number of 720. (K. A. Jenkinson)

Wearing Merseytravel livery and SMART branding, Merseybus Neoplan N4016 6404 (L404 TKB) was only two months old when caught by the camera heading down Lord Street, Liverpool, on 9 April 1994. (K. A. Jenkinson)

One of a trio of seventeen-seat Neoplan N4009 midibuses purchased new by Merseytravel in April 1995, 7302 (M302 YBG) is seen here painted in its attractive livery in September 1996. (K. A. Jenkinson)

New to London Transport in November 1979, Leyland National BYW 402V later served with
South Wales independent, Parfitts, for four years before being acquired by North Western in July
1995. Given fleet number 203, it is seen here in September 1996 with Liverpool to Blackpool
route branding on its cove panels. (K. A. Jenkinson)

Wearing North Western's Cityplus identity and displaying branding for the 86 service above its
side windows is East Lancs-bodied Dennis Dart 1247 (N247 CKA), which was purchased new
by the company in September 1995. (K. A. Jenkinson)

Originating with Ribble in January 1981, and transferred to North Western when the company's Merseyside operations were split off, ECW-bodied Leyland AN68B/1R 519 (FBV 504W) is seen here in its new surrounds in September 1996. (K. A. Jenkinson)

Starting life with London Buses in July 1989, Alexander-bodied Scania N113DRB 0707 (F427 GWG) was transferred to MTL London in October 1994 and thence to MTL Liverpool in January 1996, and is seen here in September of that year wearing MTL Fareway fleet names. It was later sold to Black Prince, Morley, in 2000, and ended its life five years later with First Leeds. (K. A. Jenkinson)

Purchased new by MTL in March 1994, and pictured here in Wigan in September 1996 displaying a Lancashire Travel fleet name, is Wright-bodied Volvo B10B 6505 (L505 TKA). (K. A. Jenkinson)

Still wearing its former operator's livery and Westlink fleet name below its destination screen is Village Group Leyland Titan OHV 807Y, seen here in Liverpool in December 1996. (K. A. Jenkinson)

Seen while being demonstrated in Liverpool on 11 June 1997 is this Neoplan left-hand-drive, dual-door N4414 in the livery of SSB, Stuttgart, Germany. (K. A. Jenkinson)

Also being demonstrated in Liverpool, by dealer Hughes DAF, Gomersal, on 11 June 1997, was liquid petroleum gas propelled Plaxton-Northern Counties-bodied DAF SB220 P10 LPG. (K. A. Jenkinson)

Wearing a Wirral Penninsula fleet name on its front panel is MTL's Plaxton-bodied Dennis Dart SLF 7540 (P540 MBU), which was only a few days old when caught by the camera on 11 June 1997. (K. A. Jenkinson)

Seen on the Liverpool Heritage Circular Tour displaying fleet numbers RMA58 and 31 is Mersey Pride's front-entrance AEC Routemaster NMY 655E, which began life in London with BEA in March 1967. (K. A. Jenkinson)

Mersey Pride's Northern Counties-bodied Leyland AN68A/1R 63 (MNC 528W), seen here on 11 June 1997, was new to Greater Manchester PTE in October 1980. (K. A. Jenkinson)

New to West Midlands PTE in April 1977, North Western Liverline's immaculately presented Leyland National 432 (OOX 811R) is pictured here in Liverpool operating the 300 service to Southport on 20 March 1999 when no less than twenty-two years old. (K. A. Jenkinson)

Purchased new by Liverbus in July 1993, Northern Counties-bodied Volvo B10B 6908 (K108 OHF) is seen here on 20 June 1999 with MTL North fleet names after being taken over by the company in 1995. (K. A. Jenkinson)

New to Express Travel, Speke, in July 1997, East Lancs-bodied Dennis Dart SLF P457 OCW is seen here en route to Halewood on 20 March 1999. (K. A. Jenkinson)

Bleasdale, Liverpool (Cityline), Marshall-bodied Dennis Dart SLF S511 KFL, which had been purchased new in October 1998, is seen here on the Vauxhall Circular 101 service on 20 June 1999. (K. A. Jenkinson)

Leaving Queen Square, Liverpool, on a journey to Heswall on 20 March 1999 is First Crosville ECW-bodied Leyland Olympian DOG113 (KFM 113Y), which started life with NBC-owned Crosville in October 1982. (K. A. Jenkinson)

Caught by the camera in Paradise Street bus station, Liverpool, on 20 March 1999, on the 35 service to Halewood, is MTL North Plaxton-bodied Dennis Dart SLF 7566 (R566 ABA), which was new to the company in April 1998. (K. A. Jenkinson)

With route branding for The New Generation routes 4, 5 and 14, and 'The Millennium Fleet' lettering on its upper side panels, MTL North's Northern Counties-bodied Leyland Olympian 0334 (R334 WVR), which was new in June 1998, is seen here at Queen Square when just one year old. (K. A. Jenkinson)

Seen in Liverpool on 20 March 1999 operating the Magical Mystery Tour for which it is painted is Maghull Coaches Plaxton-bodied Bedford VAL70 DJH 731F, which had started life with Fox, Hayes, in June 1968. (K. A. Jenkinson)

Bought new by Birkenhead independent A1A Travel in May 1998, Plaxton-bodied Dennis Dart SLF R954 JYS is seen here on the Liverpool side of the Mersey heading to Penny Lane on route 207 in the first year of the new millennium. (K. A. Jenkinson)

Seen in Paradise Street bus station, Liverpool, in 1999, wearing an anonymous white livery, is Arriva North West Plaxton-bodied Dennis Dart SLF 1710 (S393 HVV). (K. A. Jenkinson)

Resting in the yard of Maghull Coaches, Bootle, in 2002 is much travelled ECW-bodied Bristol VRT JUB 650V, which had been acquired from Castle Buses, Speke, but had been new to West Yorkshire Road Car Co. in June 1980. (K. A. Jenkinson)

Heading to Liverpool Airport on 6 April 2003 on route 500, for which it is branded, is Selwyns, Runcorn, Wright-bodied DAF SB120 82 (X782 NWX), which had been purchased new in February 2001. (K. A. Jenkinson)

New to Colchester Corporation as a conventional closed-top bus in June 1968, Massey-bodied Leyland PDR1/1 YWC 648F is seen here in open-top format in Liverpool operated by Maghull Coaches on a sightseeing tour of the city. (K. A. Jenkinson)

Resting in Rock Ferry depot on 6 April 2003 is East Lancs-bodied Volvo Olympian P351 ROO, which had been new to Harris, West Thurrock, in July 1997, and in March 2000 passed to East Thames Buses. Returned to its lessor in November 2002, it was then loaned, short term from March 2003, to First PMT before being acquired by UK North, Manchester, four months later. (K. A. Jenkinson)

Standing in the yard of First PMT's Rock Ferry depot on 6 April 2003 are Marshall-bodied Dennis Dart 40113 (M953 SRE) and Plaxton-bodied Dennis Dart SLF 40139 (R981 NVT), both of which had been new to the company in August 1994 and April 1998 respectively. Note the two different livery styles. (K. A. Jenkinson)

Carrying branding for routes 41 and 42 on its roof edge, First PMT Wright-bodied Scania L113CRL 60114 (R880 HRF), which was new in April 1998, is seen here at Rock Ferry depot on 6 April 2003. (K. A. Jenkinson)

Operated by First PMT and standing inside its Rock Ferry depot on 6 April 2003 is diminutive nine-seat Technobus Gulliver 50012 (S256 AFA), which was new in October 1998. (K. A. Jenkinson)

Seen in the yard of their owner, Happy Al's, Birkenhead, on 6 April 2003 are ex-Crosville ECW-bodied Leyland Olympian A9ALS (originally C205 GTU) and former Cardiff Bus East Lancs-bodied Leyland Olympian (C567 GWO), both of which were new in January 1986. (K. A. Jenkinson)

Purchased new by Birkenhead independent Happy Al's in October 2002, Plaxton-bodied Dennis Dart SLF VU52 UEH is seen here at its owner's depot on 6 April 2003. (K. A. Jenkinson)

Two of Happy Al's Leyland Nationals stand in their owner's depot yard on 6 April 2003. On the left is an East Lancs National Greenway, while alongside it is a Volvo re-engined example. (K. A. Jenkinson)

New to Harris Coaches, West Thurrock, in May 1997 registered P702 NHJ, Ikarus-bodied DAF SB3000 P888 ALS is seen here on 6 April 2003 after being re-registered by its owner, Happy Al's. (K. A. Jenkinson)

Wearing North Liverpool Community Wheels livery, CMT Optare Solo M850 S22 ABC, which was new to Garnett (ABC), Ainsdale, in September 1998, is seen here at CMT's Aintree depot on 6 April 2003. (K. A. Jenkinson)

Heading down Castle Street, Liverpool, on 16 June 2003 is GTL MCW Metrobus 1388 (C388 BUV), which had started life with London Buses in November 1985. (K. A. Jenkinson)

Originating with London Transport and seen here on 16 June 2003 in Castle Street, Liverpool, GTL Leyland Titan 2073 (CUL 73V) still looks presentable despite it being twenty-four years old. (K. A. Jenkinson)

Three CMT buses headed by ex-Arriva Yorkshire Leyland Lynx 2082 (F311 AWW), which began life with West Riding, rest between duties in central Liverpool on 16 June 2003. (K. A. Jenkinson)

Seen in James Street, Liverpool, on the 10A service to St Helens on 16 June 2003 is CMT Alexander Strider-bodied Volvo B10B 2074 (M393 VWX), which was new in September 1995 to Harrogate & District whose livery it is still wearing. (K. A. Jenkinson)

Travelling down Castle Street, Liverpool, on 16 June 2003 is CMT Optare Solo M850 6028 (S44 ABC), which, as its registration number indicates, was new to ABC, Ainsdale, in January 1999 and had passed to CMT on takeover four months later. (K. A. Jenkinson)

Setting down a passenger on The Strand, Liverpool, on 16 June 2003 is Arriva Merseyside Neoplan N4016 6402 (L411 UFY), which began life with MTL in January 1994 registered L175 THF. (K. A. Jenkinson)

Displaying an Arriva Merseyside fleet name is Northern Counties-bodied Volvo Olympian 3327 (R327 WVR), which was new to MTL North in June 1998 and is seen here on 16 June 2003. (K. A. Jenkinson)

Heading along Castle Street, Liverpool, on 16 June 2003 is Bolderson (Supertravel), Speke, Plaxton-bodied Dennis Dart SLF 019 (KP51 SYR), which had been purchased new in December 2001 for operation on Smart Eco routes in St Helens. (K. A. Jenkinson)

Making its way along Castle Street, Liverpool, on the 61 service from Runcorn on 16 June 2003 is Halton Transport Marshall-bodied Dennis Dart SLF 31 (DA02 PUY) which was just one year old. (K. A. Jenkinson)

Starting life with Halton Borough Transport in November 1991 is Leyland Lynx J251 KWM, seen here in Liverpool operating for Merseyline on 16 June 2003. (K. A. Jenkinson)

Wearing Merseytravel Smart Eco livery and seen here at its owner's Gillmoss depot on 6 April 2003, is GTL's East Lancs-bodied Dennis Dart SLF 7456 (P456 DCW), which began life with Express Travel, Speke, in July 1997. (K. A. Jenkinson)

Bought new by Hatton's, St Helens, in September 1999 is UVG-bodied Dennis Dart SLF V660 LWT, seen here in its home town en route to Prescot. (M. H. A. Flynn)

Collecting its passengers in St Helens, including ladies with heavy shopping bags, is local independent Ogdens Ikarus-bodied DAF SB220 H539 YCX, which it had purchased new in May 1991. (K. A. Jenkinson)

Operated in St Helens by Selwyn's, Runcorn, eleven-seat Technobus Pantheon 192 (DE52 NXV), one of six that were new in November 2002 and seemed somewhat small to need dual doors. (M. H. A. Flynn)

Seen on 6 April 2003, Avon Coaches 0138 (E138 SAT) was an East Lancs-bodied Dennis Dominator that had started life with Hull City Transport in September 1987. (K. A. Jenkinson)

Wearing an all-over advertising livery, Merseyline's ex-West Midlands PTE Leyland Lynx G282 EOG is seen here at Albert Dock, Liverpool, on 16 June 2003. (K. A. Jenkinson)

New to Supertravel, Speke, in June 2001, Alexander-bodied Dennis Dart SLF 009 (T185 KNB) is seen here in Castle Street, Liverpool, on 16 June 2003. (K. A. Jenkinson)

Originating with Liverbus who bought it new in February 1995 is Arriva Merseyside Northern Counties-bodied Volvo B10B 112 (M112 YKC), seen here in Liverpool on 16 June 2003. (K. A. Jenkinson)

Starting life with Merseybus in February 1989 and seen here in Castle Street, Liverpool, on 16 June 2003 is Arriva Merseyside Northern Counties-bodied Volvo Olympian 3258 (F258 YTJ). (K. A. Jenkinson)

Resting at CMT's depot on 6 April 2003 are two DAF SB220s: Northern Counties-bodied 6019 (N600 ABC) and Optare Delta-bodied J800 ABC (originally an Optare demonstrator registered J365 BNW), both of which had been acquired with the takeover of ABC Travel, Ainsdale, in May 1999. (K. A. Jenkinson)

Seen lined up at CMT's Liver Industrial Estate depot on 6 April 2003 are nine of its twenty-four Leyland Lynxes, all of which had been bought second hand. (K. A. Jenkinson)

Still retaining its centre door, GTL's ex-London Leyland Titan 2821 (RYK 821Y) is seen here resting at its owner's Gillmoss depot on 6 April 2003. (K. A. Jenkinson)

Named *Amy-Lou*, GTL Marshall-bodied Dennis Dart SLF 7606 (T606 JBA), pictured here at Gillmoss depot on 6 April 1993, began life with MTL in March 1999. (K. A. Jenkinson)

Seen at Bootle independent Maghull Coaches depot on 6 April 2003 are ex-National Welsh Freight Rover 374D E141 RAX and former Yorkshire Rider Freight Rover Sherpa M3 (F945 CUA), both of which carry Carlyle bodywork. (K. A. Jenkinson)

Hiding a Guide Friday-liveried open-top Leyland Atlantean at Maghull Coaches depot on 6 April 2003, despite wearing a Mercedes Benz badge on its grille, F465 LTU is, in fact, a TAZ D3200 which was new in April 1989 to Fountain, Isleworth, registered F870 ONR. (K. A. Jenkinson)

Standing in the yard of LMS Buses Aintree depot on 6 April 2003 is its East Lancs Leyland National Greenway NIW 6508, which was originally West Yorkshire Road Car Co. GUA 821N, while alongside it is Aintree Coachlines recently acquired ex-East Kent MCW Metrobus E748 SKR. (K. A. Jenkinson)

Moreton-based (Wirral) Cass operated a varied fleet of passenger-carrying vehicles, one of which – Leyland-DAF minibus L550 FOV – is seen at its depot on 6 April 2003. (K. A. Jenkinson)

Looking immaculate and lined up in its depot yard are six of Cass of Moreton's double deckers, those nearest the camera being ex-London United MCW Metrobuses A725 THV and A707 THV. (K. A. Jenkinson)

Seen in the yard of First PMT's depot at Moreton on 6 April 2003 are former PMT/Pennine Blue Marshall-bodied Dennis Dart 40112 (M951 SRE), ex-First Bristol Roe-bodied Leyland Olympian 30085 (JHU 907X), and ex-First Manchester Northern Counties-bodied Leyland Olympian 30089 (D276 JVR). (K. A. Jenkinson)

Recently transferred from First Manchester to First PMT's Moreton depot where it is seen on 6 April 2003 is Northern Counties-bodied Leyland Olympian 30089 (D276 JVR), which still has its pre-First fleet number of 3276 above its windscreen. Standing alongside is ex-First Bristol Roe-bodied Leyland Olympian 30085 (JHU 907X). (K. A. Jenkinson)

New to Crosville in December 1983, First PMT ECW-bodied Leyland Olympian 30053 (A144 SMA) stands at its Moreton depot alongside Plaxton-bodied Dennis Dart 40083 (J916 SEH), which, on 6 April 2003, was still wearing its old PMT livery. (K. A. Jenkinson)

Standing in Liverpool Motor Services Aintree depot on 6 April 2003 is open-top MCCW-bodied Leyland PD2/40 0654 (CWM 154C), which began life with Southport Corporation as a conventional closed-top bus in June 1963. (K. A. Jenkinson)

Preserved former Ribble MCW-bodied Leyland PD3/5 TCK 847 stands in LMS's Aintree depot on 6 April 2003 alongside Park Royal-bodied AEC Regent V 240 AJB, which was new to AERE, Harwell, in March 1962. (K. A. Jenkinson)

Seen here in April 2003, Aintree-based LMS Buses TIB 4873 began life in May 1979 with Crosville as Leyland National MCA 671T and was rebuilt by East Lancs as a National Greenway in December 1993. (K. A. Jenkinson)

Making its way through St Helens on the 10A service to Liverpool is Stagecoach Merseyside Wright-bodied Volvo B10L 21070 (R870 LHG), which was new to independent CMT in January 1998. (M. H. A. Flynn)

Standing in the yard of First Crosville's Rock Ferry depot on 6 April 2003 with branding for routes 91 and 92 on its roof edge is Optare MetroRider 40061 (R394 ERE), which had begun life with PMT in August 1997. (K. A. Jenkinson)

Seen in St Helens is Churchtown, Southport-based independent Cumfy Bus's Optare Solo M850 MX04 VLU, which had been purchased new by the company in April 2004. (M. H. A. Flynn)

New to Halton Transport in September 1997, Marshall-bodied Dennis Dart SLF R402 XFL is seen here in St Helens after being acquired by local independent Ogdens. (M. H. A. Flynn)

Based on the Wirral at Eastham, Aintree Coachlines sister company Helms Wright-bodied Volvo B10B L511 TKA, caught by the camera leaving Chester bus station for Heswall, began life with MTL in April 1994. (M. H. A. Flynn)

Huyton independent HTL Buses Plaxton-bodied Dennis Dart SLF W342 VGX, which began life with Metrobus, Orpington, is seen here in Liverpool. (M. H. A. Flynn)

Seen in Liverpool en route to Huyton on route 6 is Arriva Merseyside Plaxton-bodied Dennis Dart SLF 2204 (X204 ANC), which was new to the company in October 2000. (M. H. A. Flynn)

Starting life with MTL North with Wirral Penninsula fleet names in January 2000, Arriva Merseyside Marshall-bodied Dennis Dart SLF 7675 (V675 DVU) is seen here operating the 350 service to Maghull. (M. H. A. Flynn)